Editor
Eric Migliaccio

Managing Editor
Ina Massler Levin, M.A.

Illustrator
Vicki Frazier

Cover Artist
Barb Lorseyedi

Art Manager
Kevin Barnes

Art Director
CJae Froshay

Imaging
Rosa C. See

Publisher
Mary D. Smith, M.S. Ed.

JANUARY
DAILY JOURNAL
WRITING PROMPTS

GRADES K–2

JAN 23

JAN 15

JAN 1
HAPPY NEW YEAR

Author

Maria Elvira Gallardo, M.A.

Teacher Created Resources

Teacher Created Resources, Inc.
6421 Industry Way
Westminster, CA 92683
www.teachercreated.com
ISBN-1-4206-3130-6
©2005 Teacher Created Resources, Inc.
Made in U.S.A.

Table of Contents

Introduction

More than ever, it is important for students to practice writing on a daily basis. Every classroom teacher knows that the key to getting students excited about writing is introducing interesting topics that are fun to write about. *January Daily Journal Writing Prompts* provides kindergarten through second grade teachers with an entire month of ready-to-use journal topics, including special holiday and seasonal topics for January. All journal topics are included in a calendar that can be easily reproduced for students. A student journal cover allows students to personalize their journal for the month.

Other useful pages that are fun include:

✥ A Blank Calendar (pages 6 and 7)

This can be used to meet your own classroom needs. You may want your students to come up with their own topics for the month, or it may come in handy for homework writing topics.

✥ Word Banks (pages 40–43)

These include commonly used vocabulary words for school, holiday, and seasonal topics. A blank word bank gives students a place to write other words they have learned throughout the month.

✥ January Author Birthdays (page 44)

Celebrate famous authors' birthdays or introduce an author who is new to your students. This page includes the authors' birthdays and titles of some of their most popular books.

✥ January Historic Events (page 45)

In the format of a time line, this page is a great reference tool for students. They will love seeing amazing events that happened in January.

✥ January Discoveries and Inventions (page 46)

Kindle students' curiosity about discoveries and inventions with this page. This is perfect to use for your science and social studies classes.

Motivate your students' writing by reproducing the pages in this book and making each student an individual journal. Use all the journal topics included, or pick and choose them as you please. See "Binding Ideas" on page 48 for ways to put it all together. Planning a month of writing will never be easier!

Monthly Calendar

JAN

1	2	3	4
My big goal for this year is…	Before winter is over…	If I saw a mouse in my house…	A book character I'd like to meet is…
9	**10**	**11**	**12**
I love wearing…	If I had a magic wand…	I wish my school had…	When someone is crying…
17	**18**	**19**	**20**
If I were a doctor…	If it never rained…	I'll never eat…	I wish I could live with…
25	**26**	**27**	**28**
A movie I like to watch over and over is…	My favorite neighbor is…	Breakfast is an important meal because…	When I leave school today, I plan to…

Monthly Calendar (cont.)

UARY

5 My favorite gift of all time is…	**6** An animal I'm afraid of is…	**7** I want to win a trophy for…	**8** If I could change something about myself…
13 Once upon a time…	**14** On my birthday…	**15** Martin Luther King, Jr. is special because…	**16** I want to write a book about…
21 Playing in the rain is…	**22** I like to help my parents…	**23** I like to write neatly because…	**24** I'd love to learn how to play…
29 My favorite smell is…	**30** If I could live in space…	**31** The snow is…	**Special Topic** **Winter** My favorite winter activity is…

Blank Monthly Calendar

JAN			
1	2	3	4
9	10	11	12
17	18	19	20
25	26	27	28

Blank Monthly Calendar (cont.)

UARY

5	6	7	8
13	14	15	16
21	22	23	24
29	30	31	Free Choice Topic

My big goal for this year is _____

_____

_____

_____

_____

_____

_____

_____

New Years Resolutions
1. Be kind to my sister

Before winter is over _____

_____

_____

_____

_____

_____

_____

_____

_____

_____

If I saw a mouse in my house _____

_____

_____

_____

_____

_____

_____

_____

_____

_____

10

A book character I'd like to meet is _____

_____

_____

_____

_____

_____

_____

_____

_____

My favorite gift of all time is _____

_____

_____

_____

_____

_____

_____

_____

_____

An animal I'm afraid of is _____

_____

_____

_____

_____

_____

_____

_____

I want to win a trophy for _____

_____

_____

_____

_____

_____

_____

                                    _____

                                    _____

                                    _____

If I could change something about myself

_____

_____

_____

_____

_____

_____

_____

_____

I love wearing _____

_____

_____

_____

_____

_____

_____

_____

_____

If I had a magic wand _____

_____

_____

_____

_____

_____

_____

_____

_____

I wish my school had _____

_____

_____

_____

_____

_____

_____

_____

_____

_____

When someone is crying _____

_____

_____

_____

_____

_____

_____

_____

_____

_____

Once upon a time _____

_____

_____

_____

_____

_____

_____

_____

_____

On my birthday _____

_____

_____

_____

_____

_____

_____

_____

_____

Martin Luther King, Jr. is special because

22

I want to write a book about _____

_____

_____

_____

_____

_____

_____

_____

_____

_____

If I were a doctor _____

_____

_____

_____

_____

_____

_____

_____

_____

_____

If it never rained _____

_____

_____

_____

_____

_____

_____

_____

_____

I'll never eat _____

_____

_____

_____

_____

_____

_____

_____

_____

_____

I wish I could live with _____

_____

_____

_____

_____

_____

_____

_____

_____

Playing in the rain is _____

_____

_____

_____

_____

_____

_____

_____

_____

I like to help my parents _____

_____

_____

_____

_____

_____

_____

_____

_____

I like to write neatly because _____

_____

_____

_____

_____

_____

_____

_____

_____

I'd love to learn how to play _____

_____

_____

_____

_____

_____

_____

_____

A movie I like to watch over and over is

_____

_____

_____

_____

_____

_____

_____

_____

My favorite neighbor is _____

_____

_____

_____

_____

_____

_____

_____

_____

Breakfast is an important meal because

_____

_____

_____

_____

_____

_____

_____

_____

34

When I leave school today, I plan to

My favorite smell is _____

_____

_____

_____

_____

_____

_____

_____

_____

_____

If I could live in space _____

_____

_____

_____

_____

_____

_____

_____

_____

The snow is _____

_____

_____

_____

_____

_____

_____

_____

_____

_____

My favorite winter activity is _____

_____

_____

_____

_____

_____

_____

_____

School Word Bank

alphabet	desks	map	recess
art	eraser	markers	report card
assembly	flag	math	rules
award	folder	note	science
binder	glue	office	scissors
board	grades	paper	spelling
books	history	pencils	study
bus	homework	pens	subject
children	journal	playground	teacher
clock	lessons	principal	test
crayons	lunch	reading	write

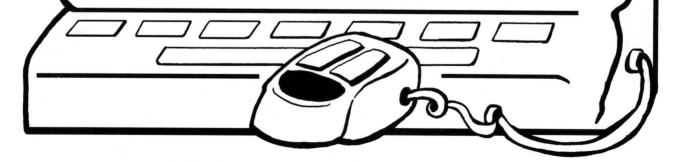

Holiday Word Bank

January Holidays

Martin Luther King, Jr. Day   National Handwriting Day   New Year's Day

African Americans	freedom	pen
Alabama	hat	pencil
balloons	horn	penmanship
banner	John Hancock	protest
caring	lanterns	resolutions
celebration	leader	segregation
civil rights	march	signature
courage	midnight	speech
Declaration of Independence	minister	traditions
	movement	wishes
discrimination	paper	writing
dream	parade	

Seasonal Word Bank

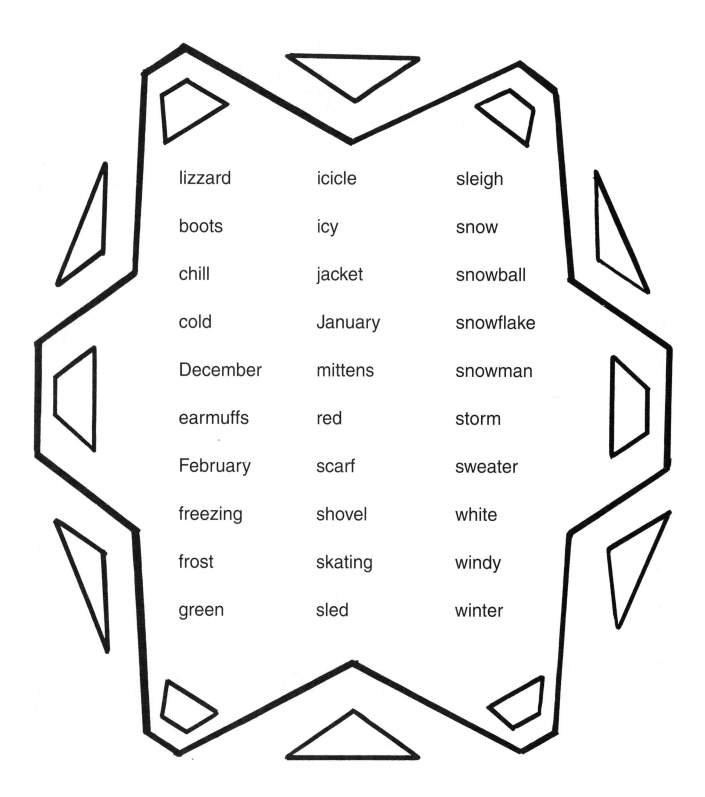

lizzard	icicle	sleigh
boots	icy	snow
chill	jacket	snowball
cold	January	snowflake
December	mittens	snowman
earmuffs	red	storm
February	scarf	sweater
freezing	shovel	white
frost	skating	windy
green	sled	winter

My Word Bank

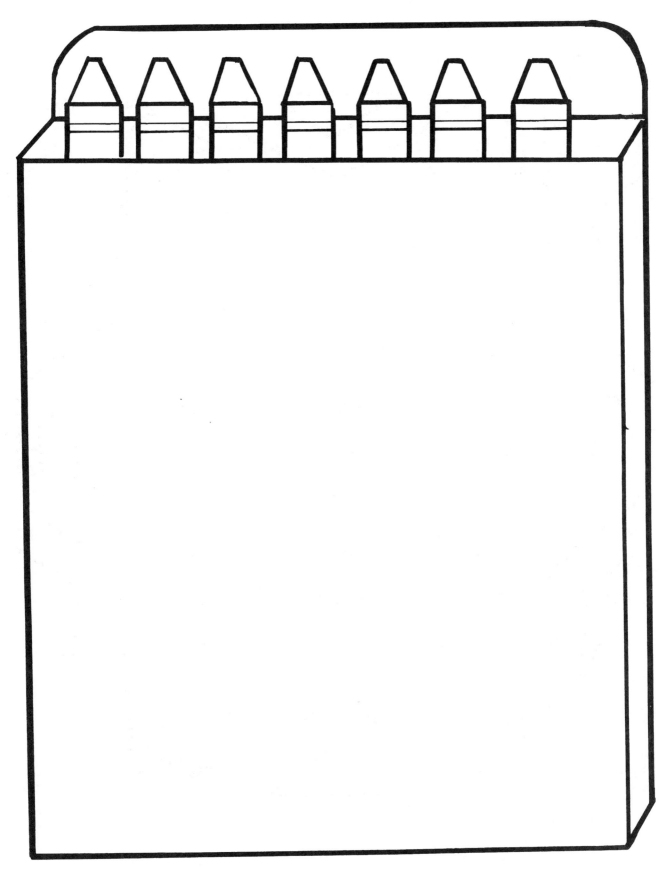

January Author Birthdays

3

Alma Flor Ada (b. 1938)

Yours Truly, Goldilocks (Atheneum, 1998)
With Love, Little Red Hen (Atheneum, 2001)
I Love Saturdays y Domingos (Atheneum, 2002)

4

Phyllis Reynolds Naylor (b. 1933)

Keeping a Christmas Secret (Atheneum, 1989)
I Can't Take You Anywhere (Atheneum, 1997)

5

Lynne Cherry (b. 1952)

The Armadillo from Amarillo (Gulliver Green, 1994)
How Groundhog's Garden Grew (Blue Sky Press, 2003)

7

Rosekrans Hoffman (b. 1926)

Anna Banana (Random House, 1975)
Sister Sweet Ella (Morrow, 1982)

10

Remy Charlip (b. 1929)

Fortunately (Simon & Schuster, 1984)
Hooray for Me! (Tricycle Press, 1996)

13

Michael Bond (b. 1926)

Big Bug Book (Little, Brown and Company, 1994)
Paddington Bear (Harper Collins, 1998)

14

Hugh Lofting (1886–1947)

Gub Gub's Book (Vintage/Ebury, 1974)
Doctor Doolittle (Dramatic Pub., 1976)

18

A.A. Milne (1882–1956)

Now We Are Six (Dutton Books, 1988)
The Complete Tales of Winnie-the-Pooh (Dutton Books, 1996)

19

Pat Mora (b. 1942)

The Desert Is my Mother (Piñata Books, 1994)
Agua, Agua, Agua (Good Year Books, 1995)

27

Lewis Carroll (1832–1998)

Alice's Adventures in Wonderland (Signet, 2000)
Through the Looking Glass (Signet, 2000)

27

Harry Allard (b. 1928)

The Stupids Step Out (Houghton Mifflin, 1974)
Miss Nelson Is Missing (Houghton Mifflin, 1977)

29

Rosemary Wells (b. 1943)

Max's Christmas (Dial Books, 1986)
My Kindergarten (Hyperion, 2004)

January Historic Events

January 1, 1863
Abraham Lincoln delivered the Emancipation Proclamation, which led to the end of slavery in the United States.

January 2, 1870
Construction of the Brooklyn Bridge began in New York. It spans from Manhattan to Brooklyn.

January 7, 1927
The first international telephone call was made between New York and London.

January 9, 1793
Jean-Pierre Blanchard made the first hot-air balloon flight in Philadelphia.

January 11, 1935
Amelia Earhart became the first person to fly solo across the Pacific Ocean, flying from Honolulu, Hawaii, to Oakland, California.

January 12, 1773
The first American museum opened to the public in Charleston, South Carolina.

January 20, 1892
The first official basketball game was played at the YMCA in Springfield, MA.

January 20, 1986
Martin Luther King, Jr. Day was celebrated as a federal holiday for the first time.

January 25, 1961
In Washington, D.C., John F. Kennedy delivered the first live presidential television news conference.

January Discoveries and Inventions

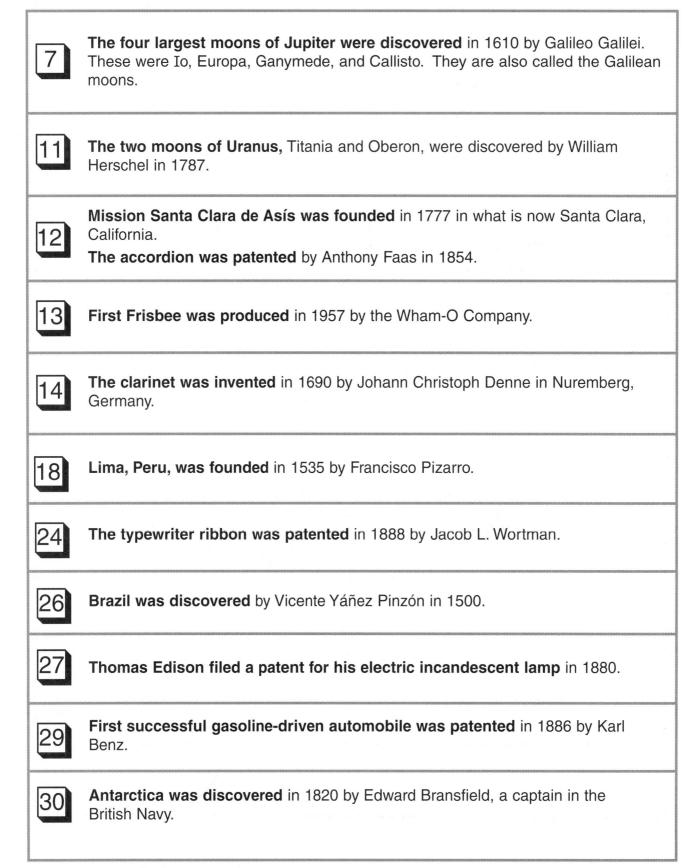

7 | **The four largest moons of Jupiter were discovered** in 1610 by Galileo Galilei. These were Io, Europa, Ganymede, and Callisto. They are also called the Galilean moons.

11 | **The two moons of Uranus,** Titania and Oberon, were discovered by William Herschel in 1787.

12 | **Mission Santa Clara de Asís was founded** in 1777 in what is now Santa Clara, California.
The accordion was patented by Anthony Faas in 1854.

13 | **First Frisbee was produced** in 1957 by the Wham-O Company.

14 | **The clarinet was invented** in 1690 by Johann Christoph Denne in Nuremberg, Germany.

18 | **Lima, Peru, was founded** in 1535 by Francisco Pizarro.

24 | **The typewriter ribbon was patented** in 1888 by Jacob L. Wortman.

26 | **Brazil was discovered** by Vicente Yáñez Pinzón in 1500.

27 | **Thomas Edison filed a patent for his electric incandescent lamp** in 1880.

29 | **First successful gasoline-driven automobile was patented** in 1886 by Karl Benz.

30 | **Antarctica was discovered** in 1820 by Edward Bransfield, a captain in the British Navy.

46

January
Journal

by

_____

Binding Ideas

Students will be so delighted when they see a month of their writing come together with one of the following binding ideas. You may choose to bind their journals at the beginning or end of the month, once they have already filled all of the journal topic pages. When ready to bind students' journals, have them color in their journal cover on page 47. It may be a good idea to reproduce the journal covers on hard stock paper in order to better protect the pages in the journal. Use the same hard stock paper for the back cover.

Simple Book Binding

1. Put all pages in order and staple together along the left margin.

2. Cut book-binding tape to the exact length of the book.

3. Run the center line of tape along the left side of the book and fold to cover the front left margin and the back right margin. Your book is complete!

Yarn-Sewn Binding

1. Put all pages in order and hole-punch the left margin.

2. Stitch the pages together with thick yarn or ribbon.